Joy
of the
Seasons

John Train
and
Linda Kelly

DISTRIBUTED BY
ANTIQUE COLLECTOR'S CLUB

EASTHAMPTON, MA   WOODBRIDE, U.K.

Acknowledgements

We are very grateful to Joslyn Cooke for
her meticulous handling of the text, and
to Sara Perkins, for precise proofreading.

Also to John Julius Norwich for permission to quote
from his mother's letters, to Artemis Cooper
for permission to quote from Patrick Leigh Fermor,
and to Edward Cazalet for permission
to quote from P.G. Wodehouse.

Packaging and Photo Research: M.T. Train

Design: Natasha Tibbott, Our Designs, Inc.

Printing: ZoneS, Milano

ISBN 9781851497782

Contents

4

Introduction

Such, Such were the Joys

William Blake's wonderful poem, "The Echoing Green," starting, "The sun does arise/And make happy the skies," rehearses in three stanzas the doings of a day—morning, noon and evening—on a village green. And from the cycle of a day it invokes the cycle of the seasons and of human life, all of them bound together and good.

In the afternoon: Old John with white hair
Does laugh away care,
Sitting under the oak,
Among the old folk.
They laugh at our play,
And soon they all say:
"Such, such were the joys
When we all, girls and boys,
In our youth-time were seen
On the echoing green."

I like the harmony in those jingly verses, no less so now that I am myself old John with white hair.

So let us rejoice in the simple pleasures of the seasons. It's the best that's on offer in this turning world of ours.

J.T.

The
Seasons

A Time For Every Purpose Under Heaven

To everything there is a season, and a time to
    every purpose under heaven.
A time to be born, a time to die; a time to plant,
    and a time to pluck up that which is planted;
A time to kill, a time to heal; a time to break
    down, and a time to build up;
A time to weep, and a time to laugh; a time to
    mourn, and a time to dance;
A time to cast away stones, and a time to gather
    stones together; a time to embrace, and a
    time to refrain from embracing;
A time to get, and a time to lose; a time to keep,
    and a time to cast away;
A time to rend, and a time to sew; a time to
    keep silence, and a time to speak;
A time to love, and a time to hate; a time of
    war, and a time of peace.

Ecclesiastes

The New Year

Ring out, wild bells, to the wild sky.
The flying cloud, the frosty light;
The year is dying in the night;
Ring out, wild bells, and let him die.

Ring out the old, ring in the new,
Ring, happy bells, across the snow;
The year is going, let him go;
Ring out the false, ring in the true…

Alfred, Lord Tennyson,
In Memoriam

Wishes

I wish you, in January, the swirl of blown snow—
A green January makes a full churchyard;
Thrushes singing through the February rain; in March
The clarion winds, the daffodils;
April capricious as an adolescent girl,
With cuckoo song and cuckoo flowers;
May with a dog rose, June with a musk rose, July,
Multi-foliate, with all the flowers of summer;
August—a bench in the shade and a cool tankard;
September golden among his sheaves;
In October, apples; in grave November
Offerings for the beloved dead;
And in December, a mid-winter stillness,
Promise of a new life, incarnation.

John Heath-Stubbs,
Wishes for the Months

Between I

I have an affection for those transitional
seasons, the way they take the edge off the
intense cold of winter, or heat of summer.

Whitney Otto,
How to Make an American Quilt

Between II

When you're young you prefer the vulgar
months, the fullness of the seasons. As you
grow older you learn to like the in-between
times, the months that can't make up their
minds.

Julian Barnes,
Flaubert's Parrot

Something Missing

I know I am summer to your heart, and not
the full four seasons of the year.

Edna St. Vincent Millay

Chocolate Time

As with most fine things, chocolate has its season. There is a simple memory aid that you can use to determine whether it is the correct time to order chocolate dishes: any month whose name contains the letter A, E, or U is the proper time for chocolate.

Sandra Boynton,
Chocolate: The Consuming Passion

The Mind of a Man

Four Seasons fill the measure of the year;
　　There are four seasons in the mind of a man:
He has his lusty Spring, when fancy clear
　　Takes in all beauty with an easy span:
He has his Summer, when luxuriously
　　Spring's honied cud of youthful thought he loves
To ruminate, and by such dreaming high
　　Is nearest unto heaven: quiet coves
His soul has in its Autumn, when his wings
　　He furleth close; contented so to look
On mists in idleness—to let fair things
　　Pass by unheeded as a threshold brook.
He has his Winter too of pale misfeature,
　　Or else he would forego his mortal nature.

John Keats,
The Human Seasons

Acceptance

She enjoys rain for its wetness, winter for its cold, summer for its heat. She loves rainbows as much for fading as for their brilliance. It is easy for her, she opens her heart and accepts everything.

Morgan Llywelyn,
Bard: *The Odyssey of the Irish*

Open Season I

Love is a fruit in season at all times, and
within reach of every hand.

Mother Teresa

Open Season II

There ought to be one day—just one—when
there is open season on senators.

Will Rogers

Open Season III

We ought to do good to others as simply as a
horse runs, or a bee makes honey, or a vine
bears grapes season after season, without
thinking of the grapes it has borne.

Marcus Aurelius

Scottish Seasons

There are two seasons in Scotland:
June and Winter.

Billy Connolly

English Seasons

The English winter—ending in July,
To recommence in August.

Lord Byron,
Don Juan

Secret Ministry

...Therefore all seasons shall be sweet to thee,
Whether the summer clothe the general earth
With greenness, or the redbreast sits and sings
Betwixt the tufts of snow on the bare branch
Of mossy apple tree, while the nigh thatch
Smokes in the sun-thaw; whether the eave-drops fall
Heard only in the trances of the blast,
Or if the secret ministry of frost
Shall hang them up in silent icicles
Quietly shining to the quiet moon.

Samuel Coleridge,
Frost at Midnight

Semicycles

Most countries have four seasons. The Sami
people in the Arctic regions of northern
Scandinavia and Russia have eight—spring,
spring-summer, summer, summer-autumn and
so on—reflecting the movements of their
reindeer herds as they roam in search of food.
The extra gradations might suit us all; winter
wouldn't feel so long if it were divided into
three, with the afterglow of autumn at one end
and the promise of spring at the other.

L.K.

Happiness

People don't notice whether it's winter or
summer when they're happy.

Anton Chekov

In Season

At Christmas I no more desire a rose
Than wish a snow in May's new-fangled mirth;
But like of each thing that in season grows.

William Shakespeare,
Love's Labour's Lost

The Seasons of Life

All the world's a stage,
And all the men and women merely players,
They have their exits and entrances,
And one man in his time plays many parts,
His acts being seven ages. At first the infant,
Mewling and puking in the nurse's arms.
Then, the whining schoolboy with his satchel
And shining morning face, creeping like snail
Unwillingly to school. And then the lover,
Sighing like furnace, with a woeful ballad
Made to his mistress' eyebrow. Then a soldier,
Full of strange oaths, and bearded like the pard,
Jealous in honour, sudden and quick in quarrel,
Seeking the bubble reputation
Even in the cannon's mouth. And then the justice
In fair round belly, with good capon lined,
With eyes severe, and beard of formal cut,
Full of wise saws, and modern instances…

William Shakespeare,
As You Like It

Prospero's Farewell

Our revels now are ended. These our actors,
As I foretold you, were all spirits and
Are melted into air, into thin air:
And, like the baseless fabric of this vision,
The cloud-capp'd towers, the gorgeous palaces,
The solemn temples, the great globe itself,
Yea, all which it inherit, shall dissolve
And, like this insubstantial pageant faded,
Leave not a rack behind. We are such stuff
As dreams are made on, and our little life
Is rounded with sleep.

William Shakespeare,
The Tempest

29

Spring

Livelier Iris I

In the Spring a livelier iris changes on the
  burnish'd dove;
In the Spring a young man's fancy lightly turns
  to thoughts of love.

Alfred, Lord Tennyson,
Locksley Hall

Iris II

"In the Spring, Jeeves, a livelier iris gleams
  upon the burnish'd dove."
"So I have been informed, sir."
"Right ho! Then bring me my whangee, my
  yellowest shoes, and the old green Homberg.
  I'm going out into the Park to do pastoral
  dances."

P.G. Wodehouse,
Jeeves in the Springtime

Daffodils

…Daffodils
That come before the swallow dares, and take
The winds of March with beauty.

William Shakespeare,
The Winter's Tale

Hang Spring Cleaning

The Mole had been working very hard all morning, spring-cleaning his little home. First with brooms, then with dusters; then on ladders and steps and chairs, with a brush and a pail of whitewash; till he had dust in his throat and eyes and splashes of whitewash all over his black fur, and an aching back and weary arms. Spring was moving in the air above and in the earth below and around him, penetrating even his dark and lowly little house with its spirit of divine discontent and longing. It was small wonder, then, that he suddenly flung down his brush on the floor, and said, "Bother!" and "O blow!" and also "Hang spring cleaning!" and bolted out of the house without even waiting to put on his coat. Something up above was calling him imperiously, and he made for the steep tunnel which answered in his case to the graveled carriage-drive owned by animals whose residences are nearer to the sun and air. So he scraped and scratched and scrabbled and scrooged, and then he scrooged again and scrabbled and scratched and scraped, working busily with his little paws and muttering to himself, 'Up we go! Up we go! till at last, pop! his snout came out into the sunlight, and he found himself rolling in the warm grass of a great meadow.

"This is fine!" he said to himself. "This is better than whitewashing!"

Kenneth Grahame,
The Wind in the Willows

Cruel Time

April is the cruelest month, breeding
Lilacs out of the dead land, mixing
Memory and desire, stirring
Dull roots with spring rain…

T.S. Eliot,
The Waste Land

Hot and Cold

It was one of those March days when the sun
shines hot and the wind blows cold: when it is
summer in the light, and winter in the shade.

Charles Dickens,
Great Expectations

All's Right

The year's at the spring
And day's at the morn;
Morning's at seven;
The hillside's dew-pearled;
The lark's on the wing;
The snail's on the thorn:
God's in His heaven—
All's right with the world!

Robert Browning

Blossom by Blossom

For winter's rains and ruins are over,
And all the season of snows and sins;
The days dividing lover and lover,
The light that loses, the night that wins;
And time remember'd is grief forgotten,
And frosts are slain and flowers begotten,
And in green underwood and cover
Blossom by blossom the spring begins.

Algernon Charles Swinburne,
Chorus from Atalanta

Careless Rapture

O, To be in England
Now that April's there,
And whoever wakes in England
Sees, some morning, unaware,
That the lowest boughs and the brushwood sheaf
Round the elm-tree bole are in tiny leaf,
While the chaffinch sings on the orchard bough
In England—now!

And after April, when May follows,
And the whitethroat builds, and all the swallows!
Hark, where my blossom'd pear-tree in the hedge
Leans to the field and scatters on the clover
Blossoms and dewdrops—at the bent spray's edge—
That's the wise thrush; he sings each song twice over,
Lest you should think he never could recapture
The first fine careless rapture!
And though the fields look rough with hoary dew,
All will be gay when noontide wakes anew
The buttercups, the little children's dower
—Far brighter than this gaudy melon-flower!

Robert Browning

Jaundiced View

Every year, back comes Spring, with nasty little
birds yapping their fool heads off and the
ground all mucked up with plants.

Dorothy Parker

Sweet Spring

Spring, the sweet spring, is the year's pleasant king,
Then blossoms each thing, then maidens dance in a ring,
Cold doth not sting, the pretty birds do sing:
      Cuckoo, jug-jug, pu-we, to-witta-woo!

The palm and may make country houses gay,
Lambs frisk and play, the shepherds pipe all day,
And we hear aye birds tune this merry lay:
      Cuckoo, jug-jug, pu-we, to-witta-woo!

The fields breathe sweet, the daisies kiss our feet,
Young lovers meet, old wives a-sunning sit,
In every street these tunes our ears do greet:
Cuckoo, jug-jug, pu-we, to-witta-woo!
      Spring, the sweet spring!

Thomas Nashe

Longen Folk

When that Aprill,* with his shoures soote
The droghte of March hath perched to the roote
And bathed every veyne in swich licour,
Of which vertu engendred in the flour;
Whan Zephirus eek with his sweete breeth
Inspired hath in every holt and heeth
The tender croppes, and the yonge sonne
Hath in the Ram his halfe cours yronne,
And smale foweles maken melodye,
That slepen al the nyght with open ye-
(So priketh hem Nature in hir corages);
Thanne longen folk to goon on pilgrimages
And palmeres for to seken straunge strondes
To ferne halwes, kowthe in sondry londes;
And specially, from every shires ende
Of Engelond, to Caunterbury they wende,
The hooly blisful martir for to seke
That hem hath holpen, whan that they were seeke.

Geoffrey Chaucer,
The Canterbury Tales

When in April the sweet showers fall

That pierce March's drought to the root and all

And bathed every vein in liquor that has power

To generate therein and sire the flower;

When Zephyr also has with his sweet breath,

Filled again, in every holt and heath,

The tender shoots and leaves, and the young sun

His half-course in the sign of the Ram has run,

And many little birds make melody

That sleep through all the night with open eye

(So Nature pricks them on to ramp and rage).

Then folk do long to go on pilgrimage,

And palmers to go seeking out strange strands,

To distant shrines well known in distant lands.

And specially from every shire's end

Of England they to Canterbury went,

The holy blessed martyr there to seek

Who helped them when they lay so ill and weak.

Trans. Sheila Fisher

*"April is the loveliest name in English, Latin, French or German
that any month in the calendar possesses...I rejoice that the
Canterbury Tales were told in April, and that Shakespeare was
born in April."
Compton Mackenzie, *The Spectator*, April 2, 1954

The Time of the Singing of Birds

My beloved spake, and said unto me, Rise up, my love,
  my fair one, and come away.
For, lo, the winter is past, the rain is over and gone;
The flowers appear on the earth; the time of the
  singing of birds is come, and the voice of the turtle*
  is heard in our land.

Song of Solomon

*Turtledove

Life

Is it so small a thing
To have enjoyed the sun,
To have lived light in the spring,
To have loved, to have thought, to have done:
To have advanced true friends and put down
baffling foes?

Matthew Arnold,
The Hymn of Empedocles

Shoulder the Sky

The chestnut casts his flambeaux, and the flowers
Stream from the hawthorn on the wind away,
The doors clap to, the pane is blind with showers.
Pass me the can, lad; there's an end of May.

There's one spoilt spring to scant our mortal lot,
One season ruined of your little store.
May will be fine next year as like as not:
Oh Ay, but then we shall be twenty-four…

The troubles of our proud and angry dust
Are from eternity, and shall not fail.
Bear them we can, and if we can must.
Shoulder the sky, my lad, and drink your ale.

A.E. Housman

Arabia

I tremble with pleasure when I think that on the
very day of my leaving prison both the laburnum
and the lilac will be blooming in the gardens and
that I shall see the wind stir into restless beauty
the swaying gold and purple of its plumes, so
that all the air shall be Arabia for me.

Oscar Wilde,
De Profundis

Summer

Eternal Summer

Shall I compare thee to a summer's day?
Thou art more lovely and more temperate:
Rough winds do shake the darling buds of May,
And summer's lease hath all too short a date;
Sometimes too hot the eye of heaven shines,
And often is his gold complexion dimm'd;
And every fair from fair sometime declines,
By chance or nature's changing course untrimm'd;
But thy eternal summer shall not fade,
Nor lose possession of that fair thou ow'st;
Nor shall death brag thou wander'st in his shade,
When in eternal lines to time thou grow'st:
 So long as men can breathe or eyes can see,
 So long lives this, and this gives life to thee.

William Shakespeare,
Sonnet XVIII

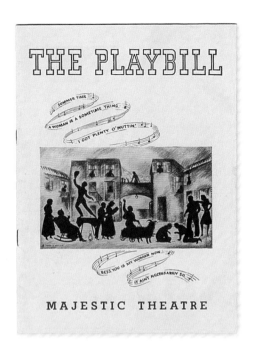

Summertime

Summertime and the livin' is easy
Fish are jumpin' and the cotton is high.
Your daddy's rich and your ma is good lookin'
So hush little baby, don't you cry…

Ira Gershwin,
Porgy and Bess

Sing Cuckoo

Sumer is icumen in,
Lhude sing cuccu!
Groweth sed and bloweth med
And springth the wde nu,
Sing cuccu!

Awe bleteth after lomb,
Lhouth after calfe cu.
Bulluc sterteth, bucke uerteth,
Murie sing cuccu!
Cuccu, cuccu, wel singes thu
   cuccu;
Ne swik thu nauer nu!
Sing cuccu nu. Sing cuccu!

Traditional
English round,
c. 1250

GLOSSARY: lhude]loud; sed]seed;
med]mead; awe]ewe; lomb]lamb;
lhouth]lows; sterteth]leaps; verteth]
farts; murie]merry; swik]cease.

Guest of Summer

This guest of summer,
The temple-haunting martlet, does approve,
By his loved mansionry, that the heaven's breath
Smells wooingly here: no jutty, frieze,
Buttress, nor coign of vantage, but this bird
Hath made his pendent bed and procreant cradle:
Where they most breed and haunt, I have observed,
The air is delicate.

William Shakespeare,
Macbeth

Laughter and Smiles

Champagne arrived in flûtes on trays, and we emptied them with gladness in our hearts…for when feasts are laid and classical music is played, where champagne is drunk once the sun has sunk and the season of summer is in spicy bloom, and beautiful women fill the room, and are generous with laughter and smiles…these things fill men's hearts with joy and remind one that life's bounty is not always fleeting but can be captured, and enjoyed.

Roman Payne

Byron's Weakness

What men call gallantry, and gods call adultery,
Is much more common where the climate's sultry.

Lord Byron,
Don Juan

July

It was July and real July weather, such as they had in Old England. Everybody went bright brown, like Red Indians, with startling teeth and flashing eyes. The dogs moved about with their tongues hanging out, or lay panting in bits of shade, while the farm horses sweated through their coats and flicked their tails and tried to kick the horse-flies off their bellies with great hind hoofs. In the pasture field the cows were on the gad, and could be seen galloping about with their tails in the air, which made Sir Ector angry.

T.H. White,
The Sword in the Stone

Salad Days I

It's true I've been led an amazing dance,
    But why should I ever complain?
If I could be given a second chance
    I'd live it all over again.
Look at the weather and look at me,
    We're both in a summery haze,
We're young and we're green as the leaf on the tree
    For these are our Salad Days.

Summer and sunshine and falling in love,
    All the sadness was foolish and vain.
It has melted away in the heat of the day
    And my heart is so full there's no room there for pain.
Summer and sunshine and falling in love
    They can cut through despair like a knife.
There is joy in the air so begone with dull care
    I am having the time of my life…

Julian Slade,
Salad Days

Salad Days II

Norman Douglas, expatriate author of South
Wind, detested the lushness of the English
summer which he compared to living in a salad.

L.K.

Balkan Summer

The summer solstice was past, peonies and lilac had both vanished, cuckoos had changed their tune and were making ready to fly. Roast corn-cobs came and trout from the mountains; cherries, then strawberries, apricots and peaches, and, finally, wonderful melons and raspberries. The scarlet blaze of paprika—there were two kinds on the table, one of them fierce as gunpowder —was cooled by cucumber cut thin as muslin and by soda splashed into glasses of wine already floating with ice; this had been fetched from an igloo-like undercroft among the trees where prudent hands had stacked it six months before, when—it was impossible to imagine it!—snow covered all. Waggons creaked under loads of apricots, yet the trees were still laden; they scattered the dust, wasps tunnelled them, and wheels and foot-falls flattened them to a yellow pulp; tall wooden vats bubbled among the dusty sunflowers, filling the yards with the sweet and heavy smell of their fermentation; and soon, even at midday, the newly distilled spirit began to bowl the peasants over like a sniper, flinging the harvesters prostrate and prone in every fragment of shadow. They snored among sheaves and haycocks and a mantle of flies covered them while the flocks crammed together under every spread of branches, and not a leaf moved.

Patrick Leigh Fermor,
Between the Woods and the Water

Summer Farming in Wartime

...The truth is I am never off my feet. Farming has got beyond me. The crisis of high summer gives me no time for lunch even. Every day more work crowds itself in. Someone gives me a cut field of grass if I will make it and that takes hours of time and pints of sweat. Then the Princess has been ill—rheumatic fever for three days which meant feeding her by hand and carrying pails to her. (She has recovered in consequence.) Cheese has to be made daily, as it's too hot to keep milk for alternate days...The pigs are as big as ponies and nothing fills them and they knock and kick me around, but thank God I take them to market on Wednesday and bring six tiny naked piglets of eight weeks whom I can nurse like Alice in Wonderland. Then all the bee-fanciers in the vicinity cluster round me to encourage my rather faint enthusiasm...My queen has done a bunk and a new virgin queen has been introduced with great application to tradition, pomp and etiquette...I always get stung—last time on the tip of the nose—but I don't mind at all...

...I have two hives now. Colonel Watson came to open and examine my colonies. I had a veil over my face and elastic bands around my wrists, but I forgot my trouser legs like open chimneys. I thought I felt lots of bees crawling up them and attributed the sensation to my imagination, well known for its activity where horror is concerned. I didn't dare complain to the old Colonel, so I carried on till I was stung on the thigh. I didn't even mind that, but it made it clear that imagination was not all the trouble. So calmly and slowly, for one must do nothing spasmodic or hurried where bees are concerned, I took off my trousers and stood exposed in ridiculous pants, pink as flesh. Looking, I found the trousers lined with bees...

...In the almost dark, I tried to get the six pigs from the pen to the sty. Three we styed, three we let evade us. Once out these fat little white congested indolences became an energetic young wild boar and O the hunting and the stalking, the struggling and the sweating. It ended just before I passed out by grabbing them one by one by the back legs (the most difficult performance after getting them once more into the pen) and wheelbarrowing them into the sty, to the accompaniment of such blood-curdling yells and shrieks that I felt all Sussex must wake to the din and brand me as an animal torturer.

Lady Diana Cooper, *Darling Monster (letters to her son)*

La Cigale et la Fourmi

La Cigale, ayant chanté
    Tout l'été,
    Se trouva fort dépourvue

Quand la bise fut venue :
    Pas un seul petit morceau
    De mouche ou de vermisseau.

Elle alla crier famine
    Chez la Fourmi sa voisine,
    La priant de lui prêter
    Quelque grain pour subsister
    Jusqu'à la saison nouvelle.

"Je vous paierai, lui dit-elle,
    Avant l'août, foi d'animal,
    Intérêt et principal. "

La Fourmi n'est pas prêteuse :
    C'est là son moindre défaut.
    "Que faisiez-vous au temps chaud?"
    Dit-elle à cette emprunteuse.

"Nuit et jour à tout venant
    Je chantais, ne vous déplaise."

"Vous chantiez ? j'en suis fort aise.
    Eh bien! dansez maintenant."

Jean de La Fontaine,
Fables

The Cricket and the Ant

The cricket, having sung
all summer long
found her groceries too few
when again the north wind blew.
Nowhere, nowhere could she spy
a scrap of worm or even fly.

To her neighbor ant she fled
For a little help to plead:
Just a crumb to stay alive,
Until the warm days should revive.

"By August next I promise you
Principal and interest, too."

Now, the ant no lender is:
Of her faults that is the least.
"What were you up to in the summer?"
"Night and day, to every comer
I sang, whenever I'd a chance."

"Sang, did you? How sweet! Now dance."

Trans. J.T.

THE ANT & THE GRASSHOPPER.

A GRASSHOPPER sat chirping merrily upon a waving blade of grass, while an Ant often passed him loaded with a grain of corn larger than himself. "How foolish you are, to work so hard this sultry day," said the Grasshopper, "whilst I sing and enjoy the sunshine without

The Grasshopper and The Cricket

The poetry of earth is never dead:
  When all the birds are faint with the hot sun,
  And hide in cooling trees, a voice will run
From hedge to hedge about the new-mown
    mead;
That is the Grasshopper's—he takes the lead
  In summer luxury—he has never done
  With his delights; for when tired out with fun
He rests at ease beneath some pleasant weed.
The poetry of earth is ceasing never:
  On a lone winter evening, when the frost
  Has wrought a silence, from the stove there
    shrills
The Cricket's song, in warmth increasing ever,
  And seems to one in drowsiness half lost,
  The Grasshopper's among some grassy hills.

John Keats,
On the Grasshopper and Cricket

Autumn

Harvest Moon

Shine on, shine on, harvest moon
Up in the sky;
I ain't had no lovin'
Since January, February, June or July.
Snow time ain't no time to stay
Outdoors and spoon;
So shine on, shine on harvest moon,
For me and my gal.

Jack Norworth

Dian Skies

How beautiful the season is now—How fine the
air. A temperate sharpness about it. Really,
without joking, chaste weather—Dian skies—I
never liked stubble-fields so much as now—Aye
better than the chilly green of the spring.
Somehow a stubble-field looks warm—in the
same way that some pictures look warm. This
struck me so much in my Sunday's walk that I
composed upon it.

Keats, in a letter of
September 17, 1819
to John Hamilton Reynolds,
about his Ode to Autumn

Fruitful Season

Season of mists and mellow fruitfulness!
    Close bosom-friend of the maturing sun;
Conspiring with him how to load and bless
    With fruit the vines that round the thatch-eaves run;
To bend with apples the moss'd cottage-trees,
    And fill all fruit with ripeness to the core;
    To swell the gourd, and plump the hazel shells
With a sweet kernel; to set budding more,
And still more, later flowers for the bees,
Until they think warm days will never cease,
    For summer has o'er-brimm'd their clammy cells.

John Keats,
Ode to Autumn

English Weather

English cold and fog and rain, grey twilight
among isolated bare trees and dripping coverts;
London streets when the shops were closing
and the pavement crowded with people going
to the Tube stations with evening papers;
empty streets, late at night after dances,
revealing unexpected slopes, sluiced by men in
almost medieval overalls.

Evelyn Waugh,
Black Mischief

October Eves

Listen! The wind is rising, and the air is wild
    with leaves,
We have had our summer evenings, now for
    our October eves!

Humbert Wolfe

Foggy Morning

I reached out a hand from under the
blankets, and rang the bell for Jeeves.

"Good evening, Jeeves."

"Good morning, sir."

This surprised me.

"Is it morning?"

"Yes, sir."

"Are you sure? It seems very dark outside."

"There is a fog, sir. If you will recollect we are
now in Autumn-season of mists and mellow fruitfulness."

"Season of what?"

"Mists, sir, and mellow fruitfulness."

"Oh? Yes. Yes, I see. Well, be that as it may,
get me one of those bracers of yours, will you?"

"I have one in readiness, sir, in the ice-box."

P.G.Wodehouse,
The Code of the Woosters

Misty November

Petrella went out into the streets which were pearly grey with mist. It was the pleasant mist of early November which comes up from the river after a warm autumn day and bears no relation to the sour London fog which rolls in later in the year and sends Londoners coughing and choking to their twilight homes.

This mist was a feathery outrider of winter, with implications of football, open fires and hot toast; a fairy godmother of the good-natured type, who veiled all the street lamps in gauze, softened the angular austerities of brick and slate, and doubled the attraction of the little red-curtained bow windows of the pubs.

Michael Gilbert,
Blood and Judgment

Autumn Feelings

...Autumn—that season of peculiar and
   inexhaustible influence on the mind of taste
   and tenderness—that season which has drawn
   from every poet worthy of being read some
   attempt at description, or some lines of
   feeling.

> Jane Austen,
> *Persuasion*

Falling Leaves I

CYRANO: The autumn leaves!

ROXANE lifting her head, and looking down the
   distant alley:
Soft golden brown, like a Venetian's hair.
—See how they fall!

CYRANO: Ay, see how brave they fall,
In their last journey downward from the bough,
To rot within the clay; yet, lovely still,
Hiding the horror of the last decay,
With all the wayward grace of careless flight!

> Edmond Rostand,
> *Cyrano de Bergerac*

Falling Leaves II

Wer jetzt kein Haus hat, baut sich keines mehr
Wehr jetzt allein ist, wird es lange bleiben.
Wird wachen, lesen, lange Briefe schreiben,
Und wird in den Aleen hin und her
Unruhig wandern, wenn die Blätter treiben.

Rainer Maria Rilke

Who yet no house has, will not build one now.
Who now alone is, will remain so long.
Will lie awake, long letters write,
And in the woodland allées, here and there
Restlessly wander, as the leaves drift down.

Trans. J.T.

Falling Leaves III

Fall, leaves, fall; die, flowers, away;
Lengthen night and shorten day;
Every leaf speaks bliss to me
Fluttering from the autumn tree.

Emily Brontë

Autumn Parting

In the sea of ivy clothed Iwami
Near the cape of Kara,
The deep sea miru weed
Grows on the sunken reefs;
The jeweled sea tangle
Grows on the rocky foreshore.
Swaying like the jeweled sea tangle
My girl would lie with me,
My girl whom I love with a love
Deep as the miru growing ocean.
We slept together only a few
Wonderful nights and then
I had to leave her.
It was like tearing apart braided vines.
My bowels are knotted inside me
With the pain of my heart.
I long for her and look back.
A confusion of colored leaves
Falls over Mount Watari.
I can no longer see
Her waving sleeves.
The moon rushes through rifted clouds
Over the honeymoon cottage
On Mount Yagami.
The setting sun has left the sky.
The light grows dim.
I thought I was a brave man.
My thin sleeves are wet with tears.

Hitomaro,
Trans. Kenneth Rexroth

*Hitomaro (7th-8th century AD) is often regarded as the greatest Japanese poet: kasei, "deified."

October Swans

The trees are in their autumn beauty,
The woodland paths are dry,
Under the October twilight the water
Mirrors a still sky;
Upon the brimming water among the stones
Are nine and fifty swans.

The nineteenth autumn has come upon me
Since I first made my count;
I saw, before I had well finished,
All suddenly mount
And scatter wheeling in great broken rings
Upon their clamorous wings.

I have looked upon those brilliant creatures,
And now my heart is sore.
All's changed since I, hearing at twilight,
The first time on this shore,
The bell-beat of their wings above my head,
Trod with a lighter tread.

Unwearied still, lover by lover,
They paddle in the cold
Companionable streams or climb the air;
Their hearts have not grown old;
Passion or conquest, wander where they will,
Attend upon them still.

But now they drift on the still water,
Mysterious, beautiful;
Among what rushes will they build,
By what lake's edge or pool
Delight men's eyes when I awake some day
To find they have flown away?

William Butler Yeats,
The Wild Swans at Coole

Autumn Songs

What is more cheerful, now, in the fall of the year, than an open-wood fire? Do you hear those little chirps and twitters coming out of that piece of apple-wood? Those are the ghosts of the robins and blue-birds that sang upon the bough when it was in blossom last spring. In summer whole flocks of them come fluttering about the fruit trees under the window: so I have singing birds all the year round.

Thomas Bailey Aldrich

The Last Rose

'Tis the last rose of summer
   Left blooming alone;
All her lovely companions
   Are faded and gone;
No flower of her kindred,
   No rosebud is nigh,
To reflect back her blushes,
   To give sigh for sigh.

I'll not leave thee, thou lone one!
   To pine on the stem;
Since the lovely are sleeping,
   Go, sleep thou with them.
Thus kindly I scatter
   Thy leaves o'er the bed,
Where thy mates of the garden
   Lie scentless and dead…

Thomas Moore

Autumn Strings

Les sanglots longs
Des violons
   De l'automne
Blessent mon cœur
D'une langueur
   Monotone.

Paul Verlaine,
Chanson d'automne

The long sobbing
Of autumn's
   Strings
Weighs my heart
With somber
   Things.

Trans. J.T.

This typically Symbolist ("music above all") stanza became renowned as the short-wave radio call for the *résistance* to rise on the eve of the allied invasion in World War II.

Winter

Silent Whiteness

When men were asleep all night the snow came flying,
In large white flakes falling on the city brown,
Stealthily and perpetually settling and loosely lying,
    Hushing the latest traffic of the drowsy town;
Deadening, muffling, stifling its murmurs falling;
Lazily and incessantly floating down and down;
    Silently sifting and veiling road, roof, and railing;
Hiding differences, making unevenness even,
Into angles and crevices softly drifting and sailing,
    All night it fell and when full inches seven
It lay in the depth of its uncompacted lightness,
The clouds blew off from a high and frosty heaven;
    And all woke earlier for the unaccustomed brightness
Of the winter dawning, the strange unheavenly glare:
The eye marvelled—marvelled at the dazzling whiteness;
    The ear harkened to the stillness of solemn air;
No sound of wheel rumbling nor of foot falling,
And the busy morning cries came thin and spare.
    Then boys I heard, as they went to school, calling,
They gathered up the crystal manna to freeze
Their tongues with tasting, their hands with snowballing
    Or rioted in a drift, plunging up to the knees;
Or peering up from under the white-mossed wonder,
"O look at the trees!" they cried, "O look at the trees!"…

Robert Bridges,
London Snow

Lhude Sing

Winter is icumen in,
Lhude sing Goddamm,
Raineth drop and staineth slop,
And how the wind doth ramm!
Sing: Goddamm.
Skiddeth bus and sloppeth us,
An ague hath my ham,
Freezeth river, tuneth liver,
Damm you; Sing: Goddamm.
Goddamm, Goddamm, 'tis why I am, Goddamm.
So gainst the winter's balm.
Sing goddamm, dam, sing goddamm,
Sing goddamm, sing goddamm, DAMM.

Ezra Pound, parody of
Sumer is Icumen In

Reversal

In the depth of winter, I finally learned that within me there lay an invincible summer.

Albert Camus

White Quilt

I wonder if the snow loves the trees and fields, that it
kisses them so gently? And then it covers them up
snug, you know, with a white quilt; and perhaps it says
"Go to sleep, darlings, till the summer comes again."

Lewis Carroll,
Alice Through the Looking Glass

On the Ice

At four o'clock that afternoon Levin stepped out of a hired sleigh at the Zoological Gardens and, with beating heart, turned along the path to the ice hills and the skating ground, sure of finding Kitty there, as he had seen the Shcherbatskys' carriage at the entrance.

It was a bright, frosty day. At the gates there were rows of carriages, sleighs, drivers, and policemen. Well-dressed people, their hats shining in the sunlight, crowded about the entrance and along the well-swept little paths between the little old-fashioned Russian chalets with their carved eaves. The old curly birch-trees in the gardens, their branches all laden with snow, looked as though they had been freshly decked in sacred vestments.

He walked along the path towards the skating-ground saying to himself: "You musn't get excited. You must keep calm. What is the matter with you? What's wrong? Quiet, fool!" he conjured his heart. And the more he tried to compose himself, the more agitated he grew, until he could hardly breathe. An acquaintance met and hailed him, but Levin did not even notice who it was. He went on towards the ice hills, which resounded with the rattle of chains on sledges being dragged up or sliding down, the rumble of toboggans, and the ring of merry voices. A few steps farther and he saw the skating-rink and, amidst the many skaters, at once recognized her.

He knew she was there by the joy and the terror that seized his heart. She was standing talking to a lady at the opposite end of the rink. There was apparently nothing particularly striking either in her dress or her attitude; but for Levin it was as easy to find her in that crowd as to see a rose among nettles. She made everything bright. She was the smile that shed light on all around her. "Can I really step on to the ice and go up to her?" he wondered. The spot where she stood seemed to him unapproachable holy ground and there was one moment when he nearly turned away, so filled with awe was he. He had to make an effort and reason with himself that all sorts of people were moving about her and that he too might come there just to skate. He walked down for a long while averting his eyes from her, as though she were the sun, but seeing her, as one sees the sun, without looking.

Leo Tolstoy,
Anna Karenina

Icy Glow

That night I felt the winter in my veins,
A joyous tremor of the icy glow;
And woke to hear the North's wild vibrant strains
While far and wide by withered woods and plains
Fast fell the driving snow.

Wilfred Campbell,
*How one Winter Came
in the Lake Region*

Snow Queen

"See there are the white bees swarming," said Kay's old grandmother one day when it was snowing. "Have they a queen bee?" asked the little boy, for he knew that the real bees had a queen. "To be sure they have," said his grandmother. "She is flying there where the swarm is thickest. She is the largest of them all, and never remains on the earth, but flies up to

the dark clouds. Often at midnight she flies through the streets of the town, and looks in at the windows, then the ice freezes on the panes into wonderful shapes, that look like flowers and castles."

"Yes, I have seen them," said both the children, and they knew it must be true.

"Can the Snow Queen come in here" asked the little girl.

"Only let her come," said the boy, "I'll set her on the stove and she'll melt."

Hans Christian Andersen,
The Snow Queen

Dark and Deep

Whose woods these are I think I know
His house is in the village though;
He will not see me stopping here
To watch his woods fill up with snow.

My little horse must think it queer
To stop without a farmhouse near.
Between the woods and frozen lake
The darkest evening of the year.

He gives his harness bells a shake
To ask if there is some mistake.
The only other sound's the sweep
Of easy wind and downy flake.

The woods are lovely, dark and deep
But I have promises to keep,
And miles to go before I sleep,
And miles to go before I sleep.

Robert Frost,
Stopping by Woods on a Snowy Evening

Shaking Sleeves

I rein in my horse
To shake my sleeves
But there is no shelter
Anywhere near Sano Ferry
This snowy evening.

Fujiwara No Teika,
Trans. Kenneth Rexroth

Velvet Shoes I

We shall walk in velvet shoes:
Wherever we go
Silence will fall like dews
On white silence below.
We shall walk in the snow.

Elinor Wylie,
Velvet Shoes

Velvet Shoes II

We shall walk in velvet shoes
We shall walk in the snow
The poet saith, although
She never sloshed down Bow
Or Mass. or Boylston*, whose
Untended lengths o'erflow
In drifts of filthy snow
And dank, miasmal ooze,
Through which, in ruined shoes,
Our merry ways we go.

J.T.

* The streets around the Harvard Lampoon were often not cleared in winter.

Merry Note

When icicles hang by the wall,
   And Dick the shepherd blows his nail,
And Tom bears logs into the hall,
   And milk comes frozen home in pail,
When blood is nipp'd, and ways be foul,
   Then nightly sings the staring owl
   Tu-whoo!
Tu-whit! Tu-whoo! A merry note,
While greasy Joan doth keel the pot.

When all around the wind doth blow,
   And coughing drowns the parson's saw,
And birds sit brooding in the snow,
   And Marian's nose looks red and raw;
When roasted crabs hiss in the bowl—
   Then nightly sings the staring owl
   Tu-whoo!
Tu-whit! Tu-whoo! A merry note,
While greasy Joan doth keel the pot.

William Shakespeare,
Love's Labour's Lost

Bitter Cold

St. Agnes' Eve—Ah, bitter chill it was!
The owl, for all his feathers, was a-cold;
The hare limp'd trembling through the frozen grass,
And silent was the flock in woolly fold:
Numb were the Beadsman's fingers, while he told
His rosary...

John Keats,
The Eve of St. Agnes

Snow on the Mountain
(first of six stanzas)

Vides ut alta stet nive candidum
Soracte, nec iam sustineant onus
Silvae laborantes geluque
Flumina constiterint acuto?

Horace*

Do you see how Soracte stands gleaming
In its mantle of white, and how the woods
Cast off their burden of snow, and how
The streams are frozen by the biting cold?

Trans. J.T.

Hard Winter

Now is the winter of our discontent.

William Shakespeare

* One of Horace's most-loved poems.
   Patrick Leigh Fermor and his companions had kidnapped the German
   commander in Crete, General Kreipe. The General, gazing up to the
   mountains, softly uttered the first line. Leigh Fermor then continued.
   The General turned, and said, "*Ach so, Herr Major.*"

Green Felicity

In a drear-nighted December,
Too happy, happy tree,
Thy branches ne'er remember
Their green felicity—
The north cannot undo them
With a sleety whistle through them
Nor frozen thawings glue them
From budding at the prime.

In a drear-nighted December,
Too happy, happy brook,
Thy bubblings ne'er remember
Apollo's summer look;
But with a sweet forgetting,
They stay their crystal fretting,
Never, never petting
About the frozen time.

Ah! would 'twere so with many
A gentle girl and boy—
But were there ever any
Writhed not at passing joy?
To know the change and feel it,
When there is none to heal it
Nor numbed sense to steal it,
Was never said in rhyme.

John Keats

Winter's End

Solvitur acris hiems grata vice veris et Favoni,
trahuntque siccas machinae carinas,
ac neque iam stabulis gaudet pecus aut arator igni,
nec prata canis albicant pruinis…

Horace,
Odes

Sharp winter is breaking up; a welcome change
to spring and the west wind.
Winches are hauling the dry hulls down to the shore.
The flock is restless in the fold, and the plowman at his
fireside. No longer are the meadows white with frost.

Trans. J.T.

The Season has Cast Off his Robe

Le temps a laissié son manteau
    De vent de froidure et de pluye
Et s'est vestu de brouderie,
De soleil luysant, cler et beau
    Il n'ya beste ne oyseau,
Qu'en son jargon ne chant ou crie:
Le temps a laissié son manteau
Du vent, de froidure de pluye.

Charles d'Orléans (XV cent.),
Rondeau

The season has cast off his robe
    Of wind, and cold and rain
And has put on sun's brocade
Beautiful, beaming, clear.
    There are no beasts or birds
That do not sing or call.
The season has cast off his robe
    Of wind and cold and rain.

Trans. J.T.

Grim Ruins

About the middle of March, the weather went sick, as it were. The air suddenly grew warm and springlike, and for three days there was a continuous downpour of rain. The deep snow drank it up like a thirsty sponge, but never melted. Not a patch of ground showed through, even on the hillsides. But the snow darkened; everything grew grey like faintly smoked glass. The ice in the river broke up before Quebec, and olive-green water carried grey islands of ice and snow slowly northward. The great pine forests, across the river and on the western skyline, were no longer bronze, but black. The only colors in the world were black, white and grey—bewildering variations of clouded white and grey. The Laurentian mountains, to the north, sometimes showed a little blue in their valleys, when the fogs thinned enough to let them be seen. After the interval of rain everything froze hard again and stayed frozen—but no fresh snow fell. The white winter was gone. Only the smirched ruins of winter remained, mournful and bleak and impoverished, frozen into enduring solidarity.

Willa Cather,
Shadows on the Rock

Ô saisons, ô châteaux.

Arthur Rimbaud

Photos by:

Sophia Klebnikov: pages 103, 108, 110, 116, 124
Nicholas Sapieha: cover photo and page 23
Mark Smith: pages 6, 12, 13, 83, 87, 91, 93, 102, 112
Chiara Tassinario: page 18

I wish my grandchildren
Sasha, Nick, Henry, Grisha, Sophia and Felix
many happy seasons.
Nonna

John Train has written hundreds of columns in the *Wall Street Journal, Forbes,* London's *Financial Times,* and other publications, as well as over 20 books on many subjects. Also a number of amusing "little books," including *John Train's Most Remarkable Names, Most Remarkable Occurrences, Wit: The Best Things Ever Said, Love,* and others, which have proven to be perennially-popular stocking stuffers.

He has received several appointments from Presidents of both parties. He and his wife live in New York and Maine.

Linda Kelly's books include *The Young Romantics, Women of the French Revolution, Richard Brinsley Sheridan,* and most recently *Holland House: A History of London's Most Celebrated Salon.* She has written for the Times Literary Supplement, the Washington Post, the New York Times, and numerous other publications, and is a fellow of the Royal Society of Literature and the Wordsworth Trust. She is married to the writer Laurence Kelly, a specialist on Russian affairs. They live in London, not far from Holland Park.